ACTUAL REALITY

Livin' the Truth in an Unreal World

by David Olshine and Helen Musick

illustrated by Scott Angle

Standard Publishing
Cincinnati, Ohio

TABLE OF CONTENTS

Cover Illustration by Scott Angle
Cover Design by Dina Sorn
Edited by Dale Reeves

Library of Congress Cataloging-in-Publication Data:
Olshine, David, 1954-
   Actual reality : livin' the truth in an unreal world / by David Olshine and Helen Musick ; illustrated by Scott Angle.
      p.   cm.
   ISBN 0-7847-0614-X
   1. Church group work with teenagers. 2. Christian education--Activity programs. I. Musick, Helen, 1957-   . II.Title.
   BV4447.O48   1997
   268'.433--dc21   96-46705
                                    CIP

The Standex Publishing Company, Cincinnati, Ohio.
A Division of Standex International Corporation.

04   03   02   01   00   99   98   97

5   4   3   2   1

HOW TO USE THIS BOOK

This series is designed to get your kids into the Bible. The lessons can be taught in four weeks and a fifth session is a step-by-step parent meeting. This guided tour through 1 John will be effective as you "know" these principles:

KNOW THY STUDENTS

Each session has been tailor-made to your students. Just as no two individuals are alike, no two groups are the same either. This course offers a plethora of opener options, Bible study options and closing activities. Use what best suits your teens. As someone has said, "Chew on the meat and spit out the bones." If you think the video idea will work, be a risk taker and go for it. If a student debate doesn't work one week, then throw it out for the following week. Remember: You know your kids better than anyone. So choose your options wisely!

Some activities take a short amount of time, others require more advance preparation and extra time in your meeting. Make a concerted effort to keep things moving from week to week. As Jim Rayburn, founder of Young Life, stated, "It's a sin to bore a kid with the gospel."

KNOW THY KIDS' LEARNING STYLES

Keep things down-to-earth for teenagers and learn to recognize their different learning styles. Teens are "people in process," moving out of the child zone and into the adult world. They are influenced by media, peers, music and parents. Adolescents, by nature, are easily bored and have short attention spans. ("What did you just say?")

Some are *analytical* learners, using their heads a lot. These kids like factual data and, more often than not, are skeptical. They tend to like computers and anything visual. Yet, they *do* like to listen on occasion, and some might even bring a Bible to youth group! Others are *dynamic* learners who learn by doing. These students like experimenting with fun activities, ropes courses or throwing another student out of the window! Some kids are *process* learners who enjoy small discussion groups and raising questions. Some of your kids are inquisitive and learn best by dialogue and hearing the ideas of others.

Strive to balance your activities so you are hitting your target. If you aim at only the analytic learners, you will miss almost 90% of the rest of the group. Resist as much lecture as possible. Kids want to interact, so mix things up. As you look over your group, consider what your students like to do. Do they love acting? Sports? Music? Computers? Draw them out, use their gifts and talents and watch them soar!

ACKNOWLEDGMENTS

• To the Olshine family, Rhonda and Rachel, for your gift of encouragement and humor.

• To the Musick family, John, Nathan, Laura and Will. You are the best!

• To Dale Reeves, editor and friend. Your ongoing confidence for publishing solid youth materials is so encouraging and empowering.

• To our fellow faculty and staff at Columbia International University (CIU) and Asbury Theological Seminary (ATS)—thanks for believing in our God-given gifts. (Special thanks to Michael Holt, Bryan Beyer, Mark Meehan and Ralph Enlow from CIU and Don Joy and Harold Burgess from ATS for your affirmation and cheers!)

• Thanks to these CIU students for their input on the bonus session parents' meeting: Brett Avery, Kirt Conroy, Hope McCrea, Rob Soukup, Ronnie Stanford, Anthony Thomas, Bob Turlington and Tina Wade.

KNOW THYSELF

As the teacher of this material, try and recognize where your gifts are, and where they're not. Some people are *not* natural facilitators and have trouble getting anyone talking. If this is *not* your gift, there are many questions and activities to help you get on the right track and stay on course. If you *do* have the ability to ask questions, this book will have one or two ideas to get your pump primed! If you are not comfortable with humor, don't force it! Try and be yourself and enjoy the person God made you to be.

Here are a few pointers on facilitating a group of teens. First, *ask open-ended questions*—those which cannot be answered simply by a "yes" or a "no." For example, "If you knew you were going to die in the next 24 hours, what advice would you give your friends?" That is open-ended. Second, *resist calling on the same students every week.* Too often the extroverts manipulate the entire time and the quiet ones feel left out. Third, *don't be afraid of silence.* Some researchers have informed us that it takes most teens 30 seconds to hear a question stated to them, then another 30 seconds to think about their answer. In other words, most teens will take one minute before they answer. Once you ask a probing question, allow for some "think" time. Don't panic—remember, the kids are processing. Don't feel like you need to come to the rescue of the awkward silence and answer it yourself!

Finally, be flexible. Sometimes the lessons might take a backseat to other issues. You might decide to use small groups or have a large-group discussion. You might use video or you might break the boredom and leave the building for Taco Bell with your kids. The best way to discover if your stuff is really working is to ask students privately to tell you how they really feel about the curriculum. Then, be prepared to tweak the material.

PREPARE THYSELF

The more you prepare for the session, the more excited you'll be. Don't wait to crack the book until late Saturday night or early Sunday morning. (Or on the way to church, one hand on the wheel, and the book in the other hand!) Here are some practical tips on getting ready:

1. Pray! Pray for your preparation, the openness of your students and opportunities to impact them with God's Word.

2. Study the text of 1 John over and over until you feel that you "own" the material.

3. Gather materials weeks in advance to make the lessons fun, crazy and relevant.

4. Make sure that you have enough Bibles on hand.

5. Make copies of the reproducible student sheets ahead of time. Err to the side of having more than you need.

6. It's easy to forget important details, like forgetting to ask a kid to be in a skit until three minutes before your group meets, or forgetting to cue up the cassette or the video. So, be prepared ahead of time! Students can tell if you are "winging" it. When you come prepared, the chances are greater for a positive teaching time for all involved.

7. Ask a few adults to serve as facilitators for small groups or provide some quality crowd control.

8. Have a blast! Be passionate about the subject. Many times we have heard youth workers say, "You know, we probably are getting more out of the lessons than the kids are." (We are tempted to say, "Yeah, we know, that is the problem!") Come all geared up, and trust God that your excitement will spill over onto your students.

KNOW THY BOOK

Each lesson is composed of these sections: **Intro. Expectations**—pre-class suggestions and ideas for opening the lesson; **The Word Explained**—a brief commentary for the teacher on 1 John; **The Word Explored**—reproducible student sheets designed to get kids into Bible study in the context of a large group, small group or as an individual assignment; and **The Word Experienced**—ideas for practical application. This is the most important aspect of Bible study—doing the Word. Each of these sections presents more than one option for you to choose as learning activities. These are represented by the ♛ icon.

Each session is designed to provide a balance of relevant opening activities, Scripture digging and application time. The allotted amount of time for each lesson is approximately 50 minutes. Be flexible. One week you might spend more time on exploring the Word, and the next week more time on the application. Whatever schedule you choose, invite the Holy Spirit to lead you each step of the way. Your hope is to whet your students' appetites so that they will want to come back for more next week.

Blessings,
David Olshine and Helen Musick

INTRODUCTION TO FIRST JOHN

WHO'S THE MAN JOHN?

• John is the author of this letter (commonly called an "epistle"). This is the same writer of the Gospel of John, 2 John, 3 John and the book of Revelation.

• He is not the same person as John the Baptist (Matthew 3:1-12).

• John and his brother James were fishermen like their father Zebedee.

• He had the nickname "Son of Thunder" because of his tendency to losing his temper!

• He says in his Gospel that he was "the disciple whom Jesus loved" (John 13:23).

• He was the only one of the twelve disciples to die of natural causes . . . old age. He died in Ephesus, which is modern Turkey.

• He was an eyewitness of Jesus and wanted as many as possible to know that Jesus had risen and was alive.

WHEN WAS IT WRITTEN?

Probably about 50 or 60 years after Jesus' death, resurrection and ascension. Many scholars date it around A.D. 85-90.

WHY WAS IT WRITTEN?

• To set the record straight that Jesus was and is God in the flesh.

• To warn people that false teachers were trying to confuse them about the nature of Christ.

• To challenge Christians to walk in purity and love.

• To let believers know they can overcome sin and Satan by the power of the Spirit.

ACTUAL REALITY

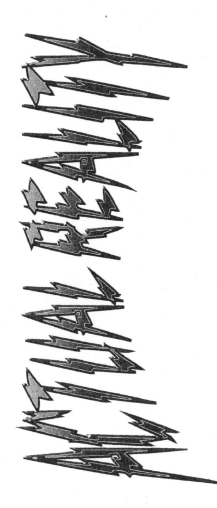

CLIP-ART PROMO PAGE

LOOKING FOR A LITTLE
BIT OF REALITY?

Livin' the Truth
in an Unreal World

 INTRO. EXPECTATIONS

♛ SHEDDING SOME LIGHT

Begin by saying, "**The TV commercial advertising Bud Light®
beer portrays a guy trying to get a 'free bud.' It usually ends up,
'No, you can't have my Bud Light.' Today, we're going to be talking about a different kind of light—the one found in the Bible.
Once we have the light of God, we should not let anyone take it
away from us—although we may want to share it with others.**"

Divide students into small groups and let them answer the following:

• **What is your reaction when you are sound asleep (in a dark
room), when all of a sudden, a blaring light hits your face?**

• **How do we allow people to influence us?**

• **How can we share the light we have with others?**

• **Why do Christians become afraid of giving away some of the
light to those they know are in the darkness?**

• **Name a recent situation in which you wanted to walk in the
light but chose the darkness.**

• **Identify a time in which you walked away from the darkness
and into the light.**

Continue with another option or move on to The Word Explored.

♛ ♛ BETWEEN YOU AND ME

A week before the session, let your students put together a video
which shows a student who has betrayed a friend. There could be a
scene showing a verbal disagreement. Another one would portray forgiveness and reconciliation. The teens could be shown hugging as
apologies are made. Use dc Talk's song "Between You and Me" as
background music. It is found on their release *Jesus Freak*. Dub the
music in or play it along with your homemade video. The video will not
have students saying anything, but merely acting, as the music does
the talking.

Or, you may want to go another direction and picture a parent and
teen arguing, then forgiving one another. When your students have all
arrived, play the video. Then, let students discuss these questions:

• **What are some keys to forgiveness presented in this song?**

NO, YOU CAN'T HAVE MY LIGHT!

Lesson Text
1 John 1:1—2:14

Lesson Focus
God is "light" and calls us to imitate Him. When
we get real with God, He gets real with us.

Lesson Goals
As a result of participating in this lesson,
students will:

• Understand that God is radically different
from us.

• Learn how God wants us to live our lives.

• Realize that God has provided ways for us to
be like Him.

• Believe in the power of God to forgive and
cleanse us.

Commit to Memory
"If we confess our sins, he is faithful and just and
will forgive us our sins and purify us from all
unrighteousness."—1 John 1:9

Check This . . .
As students are arriving,
play the song "In the Light."
It is recorded by dc Talk, on
their album *Jesus Freak*. After
students have arrived, ask:

• **What does it mean to "walk
in the light"?**

• **What does the writer mean
by the "disease of self"?**

• **Why is this "disease"
uncontrollable at times?**

Materials needed:
Video camera; videotape; CD player; music; VCR
and monitor

• **How is confession the "road to healing"?**
• **Why can it be so hard to seek reconciliation with someone?**

Conclude by saying, **"Today, we're going to begin a study of the book of 1 John. Much of what the author has to say deals with the issue of getting along with others. This relationship is just as important as our relationship with God. It's all a part of walking in the light."**

Continue with another option in this section or move on to The Word Explored.

♕ ♕ ♕ HOW MANY WATTS?

Tell the following story about Thomas Edison, the inventor:

"There was a man who tried to invent something that would make a lasting difference in the world. He tried this experiment 100 times. But no success. Then 200 times. Nothing . . . 300, 400, 500 times. Zilch. No go. Nothing worked. But Thomas kept at it. After 999 tries, the next one worked. A light bulb had been created. Thomas Edison. A man for his times. Over 900 times he went to the hassle of making a light bulb, flipping the switch and seeing no light. But he persisted. He kept at it. Edison said that every time he made a light bulb that didn't work, he discovered 'one more way *not* to make a light bulb.' Because of Thomas Edison, we have light."

Conclude by saying, **"What would life be like without light? Edison's light bulb is one of the greatest inventions of all time. So small, yet so brilliant. We are called as Christians to walk in the light and shine Christ's brightness in a world that is pitch black."**

Continue with The Word Explored.

 ## THE WORD EXPLAINED

The word "know" appears in 1 John 32 times. The theme is that God can be known. He wants us to have a personal, intimate relationship with Him. Many of your students feel guilty over everything they do, and things they *don't* do. First John teaches the reality of God's forgiveness. We can know that our sins are forgiven, that they have been wiped away by the blood of Jesus.

I JOHN 1:1-4

The readers were having trouble comprehending that God became a human. So John carefully explores the human nature of the God-man. *The Message* renders John 1:14, "The Word became flesh and blood, and moved into the neighborhood." God is not a million miles away. He can be experienced. Known. Recognized. Understood. Grasped. In the person of Jesus, God can be touched. This experience we can have with God produces three realities: eternal life, fellowship (or relationship) and joy.

1:5-7

"God is light" means that God is the absolute truth and is morally pure. There is no evil associated with Him. Those who truly walk in His light will develop relationships with other Christians and will have their sins cleansed by God.

1:8—2:2

Some of the false teaching (commonly called "heresy") was that one can be sinless. Wrong! Only Jesus is sinless! Sin means to "miss the mark" and pictures an archer aiming for the target. When we miss the bull's-eye, we have "missed the mark" of God's perfection. To claim to be free from sin is self-deception. But, if we will get honest with God, admit our sins and confess them, God will wipe the slate clean! John urges his readers to live in community with God, not in sinful and habitual love for the lifestyle of the world.

2:3-6

It's easy for people to say stuff like, "I know God" or "I love God." Yet there is no evidence that demands a verdict that they really live what they profess. By not obeying His commands, we put ourselves in a place of hypocrisy and deception. We are saying one thing and doing another. It's easy to wear a mask and pretend all is right. The solution is in living as Jesus lived.

2:7-14

There is another barometer for measuring our "light." We can ask ourselves, "Do I love others?" Although this command was given in Leviticus 19:18 and Deuteronomy 6:5, it is "new" in the sense that Jesus calls us to love all people—not just those like us. When Christ, who is the light, comes and indwells us, He penetrates the darkness and dispels the prejudices of our souls. Obviously not all Christians have arrived in their love. There are levels of maturity mentioned in verses 12-14. Some are "children" in their orientation, forgiven but still toddlers in their Christian life. Others are "young men" and growing through spiritual adolescence, overcoming evil. Finally there are "fathers" who are walking intimately with God.

◆ 3 THE WORD EXPLORED

♛ WALKING IN THE LIGHT

Distribute writing utensils and copies of the student sheet found on page 11. Give students several minutes to answer the questions. After they have finished, allow a few of them to share their childhood fears. Briefly go over the answers, referring to the background material if necessary. Close this activity by saying, **"God wants a relationship with us. That's awesome! The Almighty God, the King of the universe desires to have an intimate experience with His creatures. We can have 'fellowship,' or a friendship with Him. In this study of 1 John we will find out how."**

Continue with the other option in this section or conclude with The Word Experienced.

♛ ♛ SIN-O-METER

Divide your students into groups of three-five. Distribute writing

Check This . . .

Have a handful of students read the texts for this lesson. Pick the kids a day or two before you meet. Have each student use a different version. Consider using THE MESSAGE, *God's Word for Students* and *The Living Bible*. This simple idea gets kids involved, plus they are reading God's Word publicly!

Materials needed:
Reproducible student sheet on page 11 of this book; Bibles; writing utensils

Materials needed:
Reproducible student sheet on page 13 of this book; Bibles; writing utensils

utensils and copies of the student sheet found on page 13. Ask students to compile the "top ten" list in their groups. Then, ask them to write a definition for sin. Allow them to complete the rest of the sheet individually. When they are done, bring them back together and say, **"Sin means to 'miss the mark' and pictures an archer aiming for the target. When we miss the bull's-eye, we have 'missed the mark' of God's perfection. Fortunately, God has provided a way out."**

Ask students to discuss the following situations:

• Jamie, age 15, writes, **"I have prayed sincerely and honestly before God and confessed my sins—yet I still feel guilty. What should I do?"** What would you tell her?

• Jeremy, age 17, says, **"I pray a lot but still don't believe that God really forgives me. What can I do?"** What advice would you give him from God's viewpoint?

Conclude with The Word Experienced.

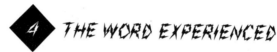

4 THE WORD EXPERIENCED

♛ GARBAGE DUMP

Begin by reading aloud 1 John 1:7-9. Then say, **"It is not always easy, but *is* very important to let go of the things that keep us from being forgiven by God. Today we want to give you an opportunity to do just that."**

Place a garbage can in the middle of your meeting room. Provide 3" x 5" cards and pencils and ask students to write down some sin they want to let go of and allow God to cleanse them. While they are doing this, you may want to play the song "Listen to Our Hearts," by Geoff Moore and the Distance. It is recorded on their album *Friend Like You*.

Invite students to come up and drop their cards into the garbage can. When all students are done, light the cards with a match. Say, "This is what God does to our sins—He burns them up." Then, quote 1 John 1:9, reminding them of God's promise.

Materials needed:
Garbage cans; 3" x 5" cards; writing utensils; CD player; music, matches

♛ ♛ RATE A RECORD

Play any top 40 song that is current. Do a biblical values experiment. Ask your students to evaluate the lyrics of the song by asking, **"Do these words express living in the light or the darkness? How?"** Be careful not to be perceived as "slamming their music." Simply allow *them* to evaluate on the basis of examining the lyrics.

Close by asking God to help you and your students live in the light in a world full of darkness.

Materials needed:
CD or tape player; recorded music

♛ ♛ ♛ JOURNAL TO GOD

As students are leaving, distribute blank paper and ask them to write a letter to God. Challenge them to share their hearts with Him about some unconfessed sin in their lives. This is meant only for their eyes and God's.

Materials needed:
Blank paper

WALKING IN THE LIGHT

When you were a little kid, what were you afraid of? Put a check mark beside those that apply to you.

- ☐ scary movies
- ☐ dogs
- ☐ the dark
- ☐ nightmares

- ☐ rats
- ☐ snakes
- ☐ spiders
- ☐ monsters

- ☐ your stuffed animal
- ☐ flying on airplanes
- ☐ a bully at school
- ☐ thunderstorms

Were you ever afraid of the dark? When?

In 1 John, the author speaks of "light" and "darkness" a number of times. Read 1 John 1:1-4. In your own words, what exactly is the writer (John the apostle) talking about?

Of whom is John speaking?

According to 1 John 1:4, why did John write this letter?

God wants a relationship with us. This relationship is called "fellowship" in 1 John. Fellowship means to "have in common with" and expresses the idea of two people who have some of the same interests. Based on 1 John 1:5, 6, what barriers keep people from having a friendship with God?

What promise in 1 John 1:7 is given to those who walk in God's light?

SIN-O-METER

In your opinion, what are the "top ten" sins in our world today? List them in descending order (#1 is the worst).

10.
 9.
 8.
 7.
 6.
 5.
 4.
 3.
 2.
 1.

Take a moment and write out a definition of sin:

True Confessions

In the last two months, I have (check all that apply):

❏ cheated on a test   ❏ stolen something   ❏ cussed someone out
❏ lied about something   ❏ kept some money that wasn't mine

What happens when we allow the power of sin to rule over us?

What does 1 John 1:9 say we need to do to experience God's forgiveness?

If we do this, what does God promise to do?

Circle the <u>one</u> response in each sentence that best describes you!

1. I confess my sins to God . . .   never   seldom   regularly

2. I know that God forgives me . . .   usually   I'm not sure   always

3. I tell others when I have blown it . . .   never   I'm too embarrassed
    if they are close friends   I tell only God

4. When I'm feeling guilty . . .   I cry   I hide from others
    I confess it slowly but surely

INTRO. EXPECTATIONS

♔ AROUND THE WORLD

Use this game to introduce this week's lesson to your students. You will need an old globe (or you could buy a cheap, large ball and outline the continents). Have your group form one large circle. Then, explain the rules as follows: **"I am going to say a word (such as 'light') that has an opposite or contrasting word (such as 'dark'). I will toss the globe to one of you and you will have to say the contrasting word by the time you catch the globe or you're out. If you say the contrasting word by the time you catch the globe, it's your turn to think of a word that has an opposite, shout it out and toss the globe to someone else. You will get three seconds to come up with a new word. If you can't think of a word that has an opposite word within the three-second time frame, you are out."**

Continue playing the game until you have only one person left. Congratulate your winner and give him a prize (such as a world map). Then, comment, **"We live in a world of many contrasts. Some people live for themselves and others live for God. Some eat to live, and others live to eat. Today we're going to take a closer look at some of the contrasts presented in the book of 1 John."**

Continue with another option in this section or move on to The Word Explored.

♔ ♔ PIN THE PERSON

Begin this activity by saying, **"There are a number of contrasts or differences between people who live for themselves ('worldly people') and those who live for God ('other-worldly people'). They act, think and talk differently from one another."**

Divide your students into groups of four-six depending on the size of your class. Have one person in each group wear the oversized shirt (either a T-shirt or dress shirt). Designate half of the groups to represent "worldly people" and the other half to portray "other-worldly people." Ask students to come up with descriptions concerning what this person would act like, think like and talk like. They are to write those characteristics on 3" x 5" index cards and pin the cards on their

WORLDS APART

Lesson Text
1 John 2:15—3:10

Lesson Focus
There is a dichotomy between the world's desires and God's will for one who has committed his life to Christ. Understanding that the two are "worlds apart" will help us live a life pleasing to God.

Lesson Goals
As a result of participating in this lesson, students will:
• Realize that living for God is countercultural.
• Learn the difference between living for the world and living for God.
• Recognize that God gives us everything we need to live with confidence before Him.
• Believe that God loves us so much, He calls us His children.

Commit to Memory
"The world and its desires pass away, but the man who does the will of God lives forever."
—1 John 2:17

Materials needed:
A globe; watch; prize

Materials needed:
Oversized men's shirts (enough for every group); writing utensils; straight or safety pins; 3" x 5" index cards

"model." Then, have your "worldly fashion show." A representative from each group should read the descriptions pinned on their model as he or she parades in front of everyone.

Close this activity by saying something like, **"We have just seen some of the differences between people who live for themselves and people who live for God. Let's look at 1 John to find out more."**

Continue with The Word Explored.

♔ ♔ ♔ WOULD YOU RATHER . . .

The book, Would You Rather? by Doug Fields, challenges kids to make decisions. It is fun and a little crazy in its presentation. There are questions like:

Would You Rather . . .
. . . have the power to fly or the power to disappear?
. . . be forced to watch five hours of TV news every day or give up TV forever?
. . . eat a bar of soap or drink a bottle of dishwasher liquid?
. . . win $10,000 or earn $1,000,000?

Students are allowed to choose only one answer and then must give the reason for their response. If you can't acquire the book, you can come up with your own "would you rather" questions.

After you have had some fun answering these questions, comment, **"Making decisions is a huge part of life. Choosing one response to a situation or choosing another response is true also in our walk with Jesus. Let's see what the apostle John has to say about that."**

Move on to The Word Explored.

 ## 2 THE WORD EXPLAINED

In this section of 1 John, the author uses the power of contrast throughout. In chapter two he talks about a new command and an old command (vv. 7, 8), loving God and loving the world (vv. 15, 16), Christ and antichrist (v. 18) and truth and lies (vv. 20-22). In chapter three John wants to illustrate for his readers that there is a distinct difference between the child of God and the person who lives for the world or the devil (vv. 1-10). In a culture that stresses tolerance and relativism, this is a powerful message for today's youth.

I JOHN 2:15-17

When John speaks of "the world," he is not simply talking about the external world of places, material things and people; he is also referring to internal worldliness. According to verse 16 this includes: (1) the cravings of sinful man, (2) the lust of his eyes and (3) boasting of what he has and does. These things will pass away, but the one who lives for God will inherit eternal life.

2:18-29

Your students may want to discuss the term "antichrist." John speaks of two different types of antichrist. The first is plural, "many

Materials needed:

Would You Rather? by Doug Fields, published by Youth Specialties

Check This . . .
Divide students into pairs and give them three minutes to list as many contrasting word groups as they can. Some examples include light-dark, small-big and love-hate. Have them add up the number of their contrasting words, then let the pair with the most contrasts read their list to the others. Award a prize to the winning team.

antichrists." These people are false teachers who pretend to be Christian. It is their goal to lead others away from real faith and belief in Jesus Christ. They have been in existence since the time of Christ and still walk the earth today. The second antichrist mentioned is a particular person. Many people believe that this is the same person as "the beast" who will come into existence just before the end of the world (Revelation 13; 19:20; 20:10—see the sidebar for more).

Encourage your students that the "anointing" (vv. 20, 27) is the gift of God's presence in their lives. It is this presence of God's Spirit in them that will keep them in tune with the truth. The Holy Spirit helps believers discern the truth, stand up for the truth and stand against false teachers.

Verses 28, 29 provide an excellent definition of the lifestyle of a follower of Christ. There must be both faith and action. When a person is born of God, he believes in Christ and accepts the gift of salvation (see Ephesians 2:8, 9). But this person's life is also to be characterized by obedience and good deeds (James 2:14-17).

3:1-10

There is an interesting progression in these verses. Verse one tell us who we are—"children of God." Verse two speaks about what we will become—"we shall be like him." And the verses that follow give us some characteristics of a person who is a child of God and the benefits available to the Christian: victory over sin (3:4-9); love for others (3:10-18); and confidence before God (3:19-24).

It is important to understand that there is a vast difference between committing a particular sin one time and living a life of habitual sinfulness. All Christians commit sin even though they are trying to be faithful to God. It is a part of the old nature. It is not until we see Jesus face to face (3:2, 3) that we will be made pure and freed from our bent to sin.

3 THE WORD EXPLORED

♛ A FEW OF MY FAVES

Distribute writing utensils and copies of the student sheet found on page 19. Allow students to get into groups of three-five. Give them a few minutes to list their favorite things. Then, ask them to go through the questions in their groups. After students are done, have a spokesperson share with everyone else their response to the question, "Can a person love the world and love God at the same time?"

Conclude, **"It's not wrong to have some favorite things. We all have them. But, God _is_ concerned if we love anything more than Him."**

Continue with the other option in this section or conclude with The Word Experienced.

♛ ♛ DIVINE CHILDCARE

Divide your students into small groups and ask someone in each group to read aloud 1 John 3:1-10. Distribute writing utensils and copies of the student sheet found on page 21. Give students sufficient

Check This . . .

Use the following to whet your kids' appetite for more:

• The antichrist is a false messiah and receives his power from the dragon, who is Satan (Revelation 13:2).

• The antichrist has a tragic wound to the head (13:3) and then has a miraculous healing. This miracle will make the antichrist extremely popular (13:4). People will worship this world leader and he will unite the world (13:7, 8).

• The antichrist will control the world and those refusing to follow him will starve to death. In order to eat, one will have to submit to the antichrist's leadership by having a "mark of the beast" on his forehead or right hand.

*Warning: Don't let yourself digress from the lesson. This view is a pre-tribulation rapture view. You may want to check out these resources:

The Beginning of the End, by John Hagee (Thomas Nelson Publishers).

Back Toward the Future, by Walter Kaiser (Baker Books).

Materials needed:
Reproducible student sheet on page 19 of this book; Bibles; writing utensils

Materials needed:
Reproducible student sheet on page 21 of this book; Bibles; writing utensils

time to complete the activity. You may need to explain that a "dependent" is "a person who relies on another for support." When an adult fills out his income tax each year, he must list all of his "dependents" (all the people under his care).

Conclude this activity by saying, **"Our heavenly Father has provided many benefits for the children He desperately loves. As His kids, there are also responsibilities for *us* to fulfill. Verse 10 talks about doing what is right and loving our brothers. Are we each doing our part as His children?"**

Close with The Word Experienced.

4 THE WORD EXPERIENCED

♕ SEEKING THE CREATOR OF THE "WORLD"

Play the song "Worlds Apart," by Jars of Clay, which is recorded on their self-titled debut release. Ask your students to listen to the words while the song is playing. You may want to read the words aloud after they have heard the song. Then, ask students the following questions:

• **Why is it so hard to rid ourselves of the selfishness of this world?**

• **What is the prayer of the songwriter to His God?**

• **What would it mean for God to "take your world apart" and cause you to be "broken on your knees"?**

Have several students close in prayer, asking God to bring about needed change in the lives of all in the room.

Materials needed:
CD or tape player; Jars of Clay recording

♕ ♕ VALUES ON TAPE

Before class, videotape clips from several of the top teen TV programs, a hit video from MTV or VH1, several commercials or possibly a cartoon. Show the videotape to your students and ask them to list ways in which each clip teaches principles either supporting or denying the way the children of God are to live. Have a student list each clip separately on the chalkboard, then record student responses to each.

Close by praying about the media's influence on our minds and the potential it has to inhibit our Christian lifestyle.

Materials needed:
Videotape; VCR and monitor; chalkboard and chalk

♕ ♕ ♕ JUST JOURNAL IT!

Have students keep a journal this week, listing the different contrasts they see at school, at work, band, on a sports team, etc. between the world and its characteristics and God's intentions for how we should live. Then, ask them to bring their lists back next week and share their findings.

Materials needed:
Journal sheets or blank paper

A Few of My FAVES

Take a few minutes to list some of your favorite things. Name the specific brand or type you love:

Candy   _____

Car   _____

Sport   _____

Ice cream flavor   _____

Movie   _____

School subject   _____

Restaurant   _____

Vacation spot   _____

Music group   _____

College team   _____

Fill in the blanks to the following song and verse:

"He's got the whole _____ in His hands."

"For God so loved the _____ that he gave his one and only Son" (John 3:16).

Read 1 John 2:15. Do you think this is the same world as mentioned in John 3:16? Explain your answer.

God *does* love the world, but at the same time He urges us *not to* love the world. Read 1 John 2:15–17. What are three characteristics of a person who loves the world?

1.

2.

3.

Write in your own words what "loving the world" means.

Can a person love the world and love God at the same time? Explain your answer.

Why does John say, "If anyone loves the world, the love of the Father is not in him"?

DIVINE CHILDCARE

Read 1 John 3:1. What name did God give us, signifying how much He loves us?

Certain expectations and responsibilities come with the job description of "mother" or "father." One expectation may be that a parent will comfort her child when she gets hurt. A responsibility may be that the parent is to provide food for his children. Name two other expectations and two responsibilities that go along with this parent-child relationship.

EXPECTATION #1:

EXPECTATION #2:

RESPONSIBILITY #1:

RESPONSIBILITY #2:

Do any of these expectations and responsibilities also apply to your relationship to God as His child? How?

According to 1 John 3:1-10, what benefits are provided to us as God's dependents?

v. 2—

v. 9—

v. 10—

What other benefits have you received because you belong to God?

LIVING ON THE EDGE

Lesson Text

I John 3:11—4:21

Lesson Focus

Those who say they love God but don't love others are living in deception. We are called to live authentically for God by breaking out of our comfort zone.

Lesson Goals

As a result of participating in this lesson, students will:

• Understand the way God loves.

• Believe that God's love lives in us.

• Realize that God empowers us to love.

• Learn how to show God's love to others.

Commit to Memory

"Dear children, let us not love with words or tongue but with actions and in truth."

—I John 3:18

Materials needed:

Video camera; blank videotape; VCR and monitor

1 INTRO. EXPECTATIONS

♛ NURSING HOME INTERVIEWS

A week in advance, take some students to a nursing home. Ask for permission to videotape some of the elderly as they answer these questions: **"If you could live your life over again, what would you do differently? What advice would you give a teenager today?"**

After your students have arrived, show the video. Consider writing some of the insightful comments on an overhead or a piece of poster board. Use this video as a "hook" into the lesson on living on the edge.

Continue with another option in this section or move on to The Word Explored.

♛ ♛ IF ONLY . . .

Ask students to get in pairs and complete the four sentences found below. Tell them that there are no right or wrong answers. They are simply to mention the first thing that comes into their minds. Let one partner share his response to the first statement, then switch roles. Repeat the process for each of these statements:

• *If I could live my life over again, I would start doing . . .*

• *If I could live my life over again, I would stop doing . . .*

• *If I could do anything for God on Earth, it would be . . .*

• *If I could say anything to our President, it would be . . .*

Comment, **"If we could do some things over again, we would certainly make some changes. Many things we would probably do the same. In our study of 1 John today we're going to look at what it means to live on the edge for God—having no regrets. Today is the first day of the rest of our lives. Let's use it for Him!"**

Continue with The Word Explored.

♛ ♛ ♛ ON THE HIGHWIRE

Share the following true story:

"In 1859 a tightrope walker by the name of Blondin stretched a cable across the gorge of Niagara Falls. He moved cautiously, going back and forth from the American side to the Canadian side, steadying himself with a forty-foot long balancing pole.

Blondin had performed many extraordinary feats such as crossing the gorge on a bicycle, walking it blindfolded, pushing a wheelbarrow in front of him and even cooking an omelette from a portable stove. But his most risky situation took place before 100,000 people when he asked the crowd if they believed that 'the great Blondin' could carry someone on his shoulders. The crowd chanted, 'We believe, we believe in you, Blondin,' to which he replied, 'Do I have any volunteers?' No one responded. Dead silence. Then all of a sudden one man shouted, 'I will!' Later it was revealed that he was Blondin's manager. Blondin placed him on his shoulders and walked across Niagara Falls. (Six times Blondin had to take him off his shoulders to keep from falling!)"

Conclude, "Blondin was a risk taker. When he asked for a volunteer, only one in 100,000 people said yes. It's easy to say, 'I believe in Jesus,' but when He asks for volunteers, most refuse to 'climb onto His shoulders.' Only one person in the crowd truly lived on the edge. For us, living on the edge might mean loving people we cannot stand! 1 John addresses that."

Continue with The Word Explored.

2 THE WORD EXPLAINED

Actual reality means backing up our beliefs and words with loving deeds for others. According to Jesus, the two greatest commandments are to love God and our neighbor (Matthew 22:37-40), which is quite different from the self-centered romantic love seen in the world. To hate another person is equal to murder in God's eyes (3:15), but to love like Jesus is to be willing to sacrifice our desires (3:16). God's love is not just mere acceptance of any theology—this actual reality is discerning (4:1-6). We "test the spirits" to see if those professing about God really believe that Jesus is God in the flesh. Your kids may not understand that Jesus was 100% God and 100% man.

3:11-19

Bigotry, prejudice and hatred are anti-reality in God's kingdom. Cain is an example of the kind of hatred and murder that have no place in the kingdom of God. God's love within us is confirmation of our emerging from death to life. Jesus teaches that all who give way to venomous anger are murderers at heart (Matthew 5:21, 22).

Love is action-oriented, not based on feelings. It produces a heart of compassion and mercy. This love reaches out to those who are lost without Christ, helping the poor and needy. In order to live out the truth in an unreal world, we must practice what we preach!

3:20-24

In their walk with God, teens need to be reminded that He is greater than their conscience. So many kids are gripped by fear. John says that we can confront fear by the "throat." When our consciences are clean before God, we can approach Him without any fear. When we come to Him within His will, we will receive answers. Challenge students to break out of their emotional jail cells. Obedience and intimacy with God are connected—they cannot be separated. Verse 23 sums up actual reality as living in the truth and in love. It is one thing to believe in truth and love—it is another to live it out on a daily basis.

4:1-6

John addresses the various teachings of the day called gnosticism and Docetism. The gnostics believed that the body was bad, and the spirit was good. Only intellectually superior people could understand and enjoy the benefits (gnosticism means "knowledge"). Docetism taught that Jesus was a spirit who only *seemed* to have a body. Both groups had trouble believing that Jesus was both God and man. John tells us *not* to believe everything we hear. For the message to be from God, it must agree with the Bible—that Jesus *is* both God and man!

Denial of Jesus' deity means that the message is antichrist. There is an evil, powerful force in the world (Satan) who gives rise to false teachers and prophets. But we have a power from within that is greater than his power! God's Spirit within us teaches us to recognize what is true (actual reality) and what is false (the antichrist spirit).

4:7-21

God's love is sacrificial and giving. The world's love is self-centered and bent on receiving. The ultimate model of love is the incarnation— God became a human being to atone for our sins. We didn't love God in the beginning—He came after us. Because of His relentless pursuit of us, we should be so overwhelmed with Him that we love others.

Teens need to know that God changes us when His Spirit comes to live inside. We are to respond to His promptings. The Holy Spirit teaches us how to love. And this love drives out fear. On judgment day, we can have the utmost confidence that we are secure in God's presence. God wants us to approach Him with respect and security, but not fear. And the kind of love that He has shown us is contagious!

> **Check This . . .**
> For further study concerning the antichrist, see the previous lesson. Other helpful resources include:
> The Meaning of the Millennium: Four Views, by Edmund Clouse (Intervarsity Press).
> The Rapture: Pre, Mid- or Post-Tribulational? by Gleason Archer, Jr., Paul Feinberg, Douglas Moo and Richard Reiter (Zondervan).

3 *THE WORD EXPLORED*

♛ RADICAL LOVE

Divide students into groups of 4-6 and distribute copies of the student sheet (page 27). Assign half the groups 1 John 3:11-18 and the other half 1 John 4:7-21. Ask them to answer the questions pertaining to their particular verses. After they have finished their work, allow a spokesperson from each group to share their answers.

Brainstorm on the chalkboard student responses to the question, **"What kinds of loving actions could our youth group do in the next week to fulfill 1 John 3:17, 18?"** Then choose one of the ideas and do it! Continue with the other option in this section or conclude with The Word Experienced.

Materials needed:
Reproducible student sheet on page 27 of this book; Bibles; writing utensils; chalkboard and chalk

♛ ♛ IT'S THE TRUTH . . . OR IS IT?

This activity focuses on 1 John 4:1-6 and deals with our ability to discern false teaching. Read these verses aloud, then allow students to get in three equal-sized groups. Distribute magazines, newspapers and poster board. You'll also need glue, scissors and scotch tape.

Materials needed:
Magazines; newspapers; poster board; glue; scissors; scotch tape; magic markers

Materials needed:

CD or tape player, Jars of Clay recording

Materials needed:

Reproducible student sheet on page 29 of this book; Bibles; writing utensils

Materials needed:

Videotape; VCR and monitor

Each group will be making a collage. One group can focus on "The Real Truth," anything that is truthful. Another group can determine "Basic Lies," which might have a mixture of truth but mostly lies. The final group should focus on "Dumb and Dumber," which are obvious lies of the media. Have each group write their title on the top of their collage. When they are done with their work, let them show their creation to everyone else, explaining the significance of their ideas.

Conclude, **"As believers in Jesus Christ, it is our responsibility to weed out the truth from the lies in the world. According to 1 John, one characteristic of the antichrist spirit is the denial of Jesus' lordship. Be on your guard whenever you encounter a person or a group that denies Jesus in the flesh."**

Conclude with The Word Experienced.

4 THE WORD EXPERIENCED

♕ A LOVING DEBATE

Play "Love Song for a Savior" by Jars of Clay. It is recorded on their self-titled debut release. After students have listened to the song, ask, **"Which is easier, to love God or love people?"**

Everyone that says, "God," should go and stand in one corner of the room. Whoever responds, "people," should gather in another corner. Give each team about five minutes to plan an argument that they will present in a debate. Encourage them to substantiate their position by using Scripture verses from today's study. Each team should choose a debater to represent them. Then, let them go at—giving each side a minute for an opening argument, 30 seconds for a rebuttal and a minute for a closing argument.

Conclude, **"Neither of you is wrong. You are *both* right! Let's go out and love God and other people like we really mean it!"**

♕ ♕ RECONCILIATION NIGHT

Comment, **"OK, so we're supposed to love our brothers, but what should we do if we've had some disagreements with someone we ought to love?"** Read Matthew 5:21-25 aloud, then say, **"This sheet is designed to walk you through the necessary steps for reconciliation."**

Distribute copies of the student sheet (page 29). This is an individual task, not a group event. Invite your students to take the sheet home and work through the guidelines presented there. If applicable to their situation, challenge them to act on what God leads them to do.

♕ ♕ ♕ TRUTH DETECTORS

Before class, videotape some TV advertisements. Show the video clips and allow the students to explain what each advertisement is really saying. Ask:

• **Is it true?**

• **Is it false?**

• **How are the producers lying to the audience?**

• **How does it line up with the truth of the Bible?**

This activity will reveal how discerning your students really are!

Radical Love

God wants us to get ready for the return of Christ. In the meantime, He has given some instructions concerning our behavior toward others. Look at the following Scripture verses, list each instruction and then put into your own words what it means.

Verses	Instruction	Your Own Words
1 John 3:11, 14		
1 John 3:12, 15		
1 John 3:16		
1 John 3:17, 18		

Why do you think hatred is considered as bad as murder?

What are three practical ways you can lay down your life for other Christians?
1.
2.
3.

What kinds of loving actions could our youth group do in the next week to fulfill 1 John 3:17, 18?

Verses	Instruction	Your Own Words
1 John 4:7, 8, 11		
1 John 4:15		
1 John 4:17		
1 John 4:19-21		

How can I love someone that I really don't like?

Does "love one another" mean that I have to like everyone? Explain your answer.

RECONCILIATION NIGHT

1. READ MATTHEW 5:21–25 AND MATTHEW 18:21–35.

2. IDENTIFY THE PERSON:

_____ (initials) of the person who has something against you

_____ (initials) of the person that you have sinned against or hurt

3. GAME PLAN

Think through your options and check the action which you plan to take.

- ☐ I will seek to mend the relationship by calling this person on the phone.
- ☐ I will go and visit this person face-to-face and seek reconciliation.
- ☐ I will write a letter and ask for forgiveness.
- ☐ Other _____

4. SOME PRACTICAL TIPS

- Don't blame the other person. Share how you feel.
- Don't make excuses for yourself.
- 'Fess up. Confession is good. Say the words, "I am sorry."
- Timing is everything. Four o'clock in the morning might be a little unsettling!
- Letter writing has its problems. Sometimes people misinterpret a letter because the reader cannot see the body language of the writer, nor the tone of the letter.
- Use "I" statements, not "you." "I felt like . . ." is a statement of personal ownership. "You made me . . ." is an attack on the other person.

5. WHATEVER METHOD YOU CHOOSE, GO HUMBLY AND HONESTLY, EXPECTING THE RELATIONSHIP TO GET BACK ON TRACK.

6. WHEN YOU MAKE THE DECISION TO CORRECT THE CONFLICT, BE PRAYED UP. ASK GOD TO GO BEFORE YOU.

7. AHEAD OF TIME, WRITE OUT WHAT YOU REALLY WANT TO SAY. THINK CAREFULLY ABOUT THE WORDS YOU WANT TO USE SO THAT THEY DO NOT COME OUT EXPLOSIVELY.

8. GO AND DO IT!

1 *INTRO. EXPECTATIONS*

♔ "FATHER, MAY I?"

Begin by dividing students into teams of 4-8, depending on the size of your group. Share the rules of the game:

"Like the childhood game, 'Mother, May I,' I will give commands to the first person in each group. If the person chooses to participate in the command, he should respond with the question, 'Father, may I?' and I will say, 'Yes, you may.' The student must then follow through with the command. The first team to complete the command gets a point. Then, two different students will come up and receive another command. We'll continue until all of the commands have been carried out."

The way to make this game a big hit is to think of crazy commands for the students to carry out. Here are some examples:

• Have students eat a jar of baby food—something gross like pureed spinach.

• Have students kiss the foot of each team member.

• Have students sing, "Row, row, row your boat" while sitting on someone's back, rowing as if they were in a boat.

• Have students cluck and walk like a chicken. The first one who clucks and walks to a certain point in the room wins.

• Have students eat an onion or a lemon.

• Have students chew three pieces of bubble gum and blow a bubble.

Conclude this activity by saying, **"Fortunately for us, our heavenly Father doesn't ask us to do such crazy things. But He *does* ask us to obey His commands. Loving God and obeying Him go hand in hand. Let's see what John has to say as we conclude our study on his first epistle."**

Continue with another option in this section or move on to The Word Explored.

♔ ♔ LET IT SNOW, LET IT SNOW, LET IT SNOW

Divide your meeting room into two halves by drawing a line on the floor with masking tape. Put half of the students on one side of the

LOVE AND OBEY: THERE'S NO OTHER WAY

Lesson Text

I John 5:1-21

Lesson Focus

Love and obedience go hand in hand for the person who has committed his life to Christ. While it may seem difficult to obey God's commands, He promises that they are not burdensome.

Lesson Goals

As a result of participating in this lesson, students will:

• Understand that to obey God is to love God.

• Learn what it means to be a child of God and have the assurance of eternal life.

• Realize that God gives us the power to overcome the world.

• Believe that when we pray according to His will, God hears us.

Commit to Memory

"I write these things to you who believe in the name of the Son of God so that you may know that you have eternal life."—I John 5:13

Materials needed:
Various food items

Materials needed:
Masking tape; cotton balls; whistle; gift certificates

room and the other half on the opposite side. Sprinkle cotton balls all over the floor. The more cotton balls the better. Then, ask your students to get down on their hands and knees. When you blow the whistle, they are to throw as many cotton balls to the other side as possible. Their battle should look like a giant snowball fight. When you blow the whistle again, the game is over. Survey the damage to see who has the most cotton balls in their half of the room—they're the losing team. You may want to play this several times. Award the winners gift certificates for free snow cones.

Afterward, comment, **"As we wind up our study of 1 John, today we're going to see that Christians can 'overcome the world' by their faith. Often the battle seems as though it will never stop. Let's see just how much God is on our side."**

Continue with another option in this section or move on to The Word Explored.

♕ ♕ ♕ You Must Choose Wisely

Ahead of time, design your meeting room the following way: Attach a huge "+" sign signifying "yes" on one wall of the room. On the opposite wall attach a "—" signifying "no." Tell the students they must choose one side of the room or the other to indicate their response to the following statements concerning whether or not they are "God's will." Tell them they *must* choose "yes" or "no" and that they may not stand in between the two choices. After each statement, allow a student from each side to defend his position.

Here are some possible prayer scenarios you can use (feel free to add to the list):

 • **It is God's will that all people become His children.**
 • **It is God's will that everyone be happy.**
 • **It is God's will that people in poor countries not starve to death.**
 • **It is God's will that parents not divorce.**
 • **It is God's will that the school cafeteria manager get fired and be replaced by (their favorite fast-food restaurant).**

After you have finished the activity, comment, **"As we conclude our study of 1 John, one of the things we will discuss is God's will. John says our prayers will be answered if we pray within God's will."**

Continue with The Word Explored.

 ## THE WORD EXPLAINED

I JOHN 5:1-5

Becoming a Christian means becoming a part of a new family— the family of believers. As Christians, we show that we love God and are His children by obeying His commands. The two go hand in hand. Just as in a biological family the members are to respect and care for one another, so too, in the family of God, we are to love each other.

Obeying God's commands are not to be burdensome or heavy. John encourages us that if we persevere in keeping God's commands, we will—through faith (v. 4)—overcome the world.

Materials needed:

Two pieces of poster board; magic markers; masking tape

5:6-12

The phrase "came by water and blood" may refer to the water baptism of Jesus and the blood that He shed on the cross. These two events are foundational to the Christian faith. It was during Christ's baptism that God's Spirit announced, "'This is my Son, whom I love; with him I am well pleased'" (Matthew 3:17). And it was His blood that allowed us to be joint-heirs with Jesus as children of God.

Eternal life is freely given to anyone who has the Son (v. 12). John says that it is God who has given us eternal life and that this life is in His Son, Jesus.

5:13-21

How can you know that you have eternal life? In verse 13, John says this is exactly why he wrote this first letter—so that we may *know!* Eternal life is often thought of as an event that occurs when we die. But eternal life begins the moment a person believes in the name of the Son of God. This life in Heaven with Jesus is not based on feelings, but on the fact that God promised this gift to His children.

The emphasis on approaching God and asking Him for "anything" (v. 14) is not based on what we wish for, but according to God's will. This type of request will result in God hearing us (v. 15) and receiving our prayer. The focus is on what *God* wants for us rather than what *we* want for ourselves. Rest assured that He knows what we really need better than we know ourselves!

Verses 16, 17 once again deal with the accountability of believers to one another—as brother to brother and sister to sister. If you see your brother or sister commit a sin, pray for him or her. But a special situation exists when you see a believer commit a "sin that leads to death." This sin is to be dealt with differently than simply by praying. There are several places in the Bible that speak of this sin that leads to death. These include: Mark 3:29; Acts 5:1-11; 1 Corinthians 11:27-30; Hebrew 6:4-6; and 2 Peter 2:20-22. You may want to research this with your students briefly, but don't allow the discussion to steer you away from the main point of this lesson—that we are called to an exciting life in the Son, characterized by love and obedience.

 THE WORD EXPLORED

♛ LOVE RULES

Begin this activity by saying, **"Many of your friends say that different professional sports teams or music groups or movies 'rule'! In our study today, the apostle John talks about some of the 'rules' regarding the life of love we have in Jesus Christ. Let's take a look at them."**

Distribute copies of the student sheet (page 35) and writing utensils. Allow students to work on the sheet individually. Refer to the background information in discussing the interconnectedness of belief, love and obedience.

After students have finished working, conclude by saying, **"God's love rules! He is so incredibly magnificent and perfect, that He guarantees we will live with Him forever—if we choose to follow**

Materials needed:
Reproducible student sheet on page 35 of this book; Bibles; writing utensils; CD or tape player; music

Check This . . .
As students are working, play some background music. One good choice would be "Cry for Love," recorded by Michael W. Smith on his album *I'll Lead You Home.*

Him now. If you couldn't answer 'yes' to the last question on the sheet, I would be glad to talk with you more about it. That's why I'm here."

Continue with the other option in this section or conclude with The Word Experienced.

♔ ♔ MY CHALLENGE TO OUR YOUTH GROUP

Distribute copies of the student sheet found on page 37 of this book. Have group members write down one to three passages from 1 John 5:1-21 that they feel are most imperative for the group to hear. Let your students spend 10-15 minutes alone and then gather them back together.

Ask for several students to read the Scriptures they chose and give their own contemporary interpretations. Let the impact of this time sink in. This is the students' chance to admonish one another for a display of hypocrisy or a lack of love, present a challenge to pray or share some encouraging word.

Conclude with The Word Experienced.

4   THE WORD EXPERIENCED

♔ JUST PRAY IT

This experience will encourage your students to pray. Distribute the paper or journal sheets and pencils. Instruct students as follows: **"This week you're going to have an opportunity to keep a record of your prayer requests. Make three columns on your paper. At the top of one column, write 'prayer request.' Next to it, write 'reflection.' In this space you'll be able to think about whether this prayer request is something God should do, could do or 'wills' for your life. In the third column, write 'date answered.' Keep track of when and how these prayer requests are answered."**

The next time you get together, let students who feel comfortable share their experiences. Their findings may lead into a good discussion concerning why God seems to answer some requests "yes," but others "no."

♔ ♔ PRAYING AS ONE

Listen to Michael W. Smith's song "As It Is in Heaven" from the CD *I'll Lead You Home.* This is a song of the Lord's prayer found in Matthew 6:9-15. Discuss why Jesus would choose these principles to be a model for how He wants us to pray. Then form a circle, join hands and close the time by saying the Lord's prayer in unison.

Materials needed:

Reproducible student sheet on page 37 of this book; Bibles; writing utensils

Materials needed:

Blank paper or journal sheets; writing utensils

Materials needed:

CD or tape player; Michael W. Smith recording

Check This . . .
An upbeat song that deals with talking with God is "We Talk to the Lord," by The World Wide Message Tribe. It is recorded on their album *We Don't Get What We Deserve.*

LOVE RULES

Rank each of the following rules from 1-5 according to how important they are in expressing your love for God (1 means not important at all, 5 means very important).

____ Brushing your teeth two times a day
____ Obeying your parent(s)
____ Forgiving one who has wronged you
____ Driving the speed limit
____ Saving sex for marriage
____ Making good grades
____ Always telling the truth

Read 1 John 5:1-5. How important are belief, love and obedience? How are they interconnected?

BELIEF—

LOVE—

OBEDIENCE—

Read 1 John 5:14, 15. According to these verses, we can have confidence whenever we approach God in prayer. That's part of His love for us. What is our confidence based on?

Take a moment to evaluate your prayer life. Do you pray according to these guidelines? Why or why not?

Assurance means a guarantee, a promise, a "sure thing." Check your top three choices of things that give you confidence or assurance in this life.

☐ friends   ☐ popularity   ☐ knowledge   ☐ sports
☐ family   ☐ money   ☐ God   ☐ mouthwash
☐ a mind-altering substance   ☐ other_____

John shares his reason for writing this letter in 1 John 5:13. What is that reason?

Can you say that you <u>know</u> you have eternal life?

MY CHALLENGE TO OUR YOUTH GROUP

1 John 5:1–21

Scripture #1:
My Contemporary Interpretation:

Scripture #2:
My Contemporary Interpretation:

Scripture #3:
My Contemporary Interpretation:

A PARENTS' MEETING

COMMUNICATION: HOW TO REALLY TALK WITH YOUR TEEN

Text
Selected verses from I John

Focus
A 75-minute seminar for parents of preteens and teenagers

Outline:
1. Purpose of Seminar
2. Steps of Preparation
3. Step-by-Step Meeting Plan
4. Resources

PURPOSE OF SEMINAR

The objective is to invite parents of preteens (grades 4-6) and teens (grades 7-12) to a relaxing 75-minute seminar that will provide three strategies for effective communication within their home life. This seminar will be fast-paced with small group discussion, video clips and some practical teaching on communication skills.

STEPS OF PREPARATION

Preparation is the most crucial ingredient for a successful meeting. Prior preparation prevents poor performance! Commit yourself to "beating the bushes" so that you'll have a good turnout. If you've never led a parent meeting before, don't panic. Here are some questions to ask as you plan your meeting. The answers will vary based on your intended design, whom you want to reach and your budget limitations.

A. WHERE WILL I HOLD THE MEETING?
You may want to have it in the church building, in the fellowship hall or in a neutral site off campus to reach more unchurched families.

B. HOW MANY PEOPLE DO I WANT TO ATTEND THE SEMINAR?
If this is your first attempt at any kind of parent ministry, consider keeping it small and intimate. Whatever your guesstimate, err to the side of having fewer than you think. If you hold the meeting in a sanctuary that seats 800 and only 35 show up, people will feel that there's not much happening. If you hope to have 80 attend, set up a room that holds 75! If you think ten will come, clean out the janitor's closet.

C. WHAT TYPE OF AUDIENCE AM I TRYING TO REACH?
You will need to determine: Is it for my church only? Do I want other churches involved? Do I plan to reach out to non-churched parents? Will the group be primarily lower, middle or upper class? Some groups have held seminars like this in a neutral spot, like a hotel, to reach out to unchurched parents.

D. How will I advertise?

Will it be in the church bulletin only? The local newspaper? Why not design a professional brochure that could be placed in area supermarkets, real estate avenues or home mailers? What about radio ads, TV spots, flyers and posters? And, don't forget word of mouth!

E. When is the best time to have it?

Check the church and school calendars first! Obviously you'll want to avoid holidays. Work around big events, like football games, that would pull parents away. Some prefer Saturday mornings, others Saturday night. Perhaps the Sunday school hour is your best bet. Choose the right time and season for you, set the date and go for it.

F. How much will it cost?

If you have a budget, there are considerable costs in publicity. You might want to offer a Saturday or Sunday night meal, and charge a small fee for the dinner. This meeting is designed to be self-sufficient without having to bring in a speaker. It also depends on how much you want to do. If you have a meal or snacks, someone is going to have to pay. In general, it can often be done for less than $300.

G. Who will help me?

Using volunteers is the only way to fly. Create a team of people who will select the date, organize the food, determine the site, costs, advertising and other details. Choose some parents from the church because their ownership in the event will help bring other parents.

H. When will we begin advertising?

It depends on your community. Some places, six weeks is plenty. In other places, six months is not soon enough.

I. What kinds of equipment and supplies will I need?

You will need: a solid microphone system, TV, VCR, overhead projector and session handouts provided in this book (therefore, you'll need a copier). One handout is a transparency for the overhead projector. Have name tags for those who attend the seminar. You'll also need signs indicating where the meeting will be held, a registration table manned by a few volunteers and a table of helpful resources.

J. What resources do I need?

See the recommended list on page 43. Your local Christian bookstore might be willing to order the books and run the "bookstore" for you on site. They may want to offer some discounts and give away a few books because you have just brought them some business!

K. How will we arrange the room?

Let the planning team decide, then delegate it to other parents.

L. How about a prayer team?

You are right on track! Without prayer, the event will not have the power it needs. Get some prayer warriors on the team and ask God to bring those who really need to be present.

If you publicize that the meeting is 75 minutes, be faithful to honor the time frame. If you're not careful, discussions can go over-time. Do your best to start and end on time. You can shorten some of the activities to make the session last 60 minutes if you need to.

♛ OPENER (about 15 minutes)
A. SMALL GROUP EXERCISE #1 (about 5 minutes)

Welcome everyone to the seminar. Introduce yourself and the topic. Ask those in attendance to break into small groups of three or four. Explain that the facilitator of each group (whose role is to help others share) is the one with the longest hair. Each person should give their names, and then give the name, age and a phrase that best describes their child (or children). For example, "I have a six year old, named Emily, who is funny, and a 16 year old, named Jonathan, who loves basketball." After they have finished this simple exercise, have them remain in their groups. Move right into the next activity.

B. WHEN I WAS A TEEN (IN THE DARK AGES) (about 10 minutes)

Distribute copies of the handout on page 44 as well as writing utensils. Ask participants to answer the questions, then share their responses with everyone in their group. After they have finished the first four questions, bring them back together into a large group.

Materials needed:
Reproducible handout on page 44 of this book; writing utensils

You will need to monitor the time and keep the groups on track. It is okay to say, "time's up," even if they have not all finished. It is better to frustrate them by not letting some finish than have two or three groups bored as they wait for other groups to complete their assignments.

♛ ♛ GROUP DISCUSSION, VIDEO AND LECTURE (about 60 minutes)

Have the attendees name some ingredients that make up good communication. As they name them, make a list on an overhead transparency or the chalkboard. They will probably say things like good eye contact, affirmation and body language.

Materials needed:
Overhead projector; chalkboard and chalk; handout on page 44 of this book; writing utensils; transparency on page 45 of this book; videos; VCR; TV

Comment, **"The primary purpose of this seminar is to help us communicate better with our kids. There are three strategies that will help us meet these objectives—(1) Learn to listen so your teen will speak, (2) Learn to talk so your teen will listen and (3) Learn to read your teen's 'rhythm and moods.'"**

Display the transparency "Strategies for Great Communication." (Before the session you will need to run a transparency through your copy machine, while copying page 45 of this book.)

Start with strategy #1—Learn to listen so your teen will speak.

Say, **"Most surveys suggest that the number one complaint from teens about their parents is that they don't listen to them. When parents of teens were surveyed, they said their number one desire is that they could listen in a way that their teen would really talk. So how do we do this?"**

"I'd like you to pair up with someone and complete the 'Who, Me . . . Communicate?' part of the handout." Let them share with their partners how they filled in the blanks of the first two statements:

1. I wish my teen would be able to discuss _____ (subject) with me.

2. I wish I could discuss _____ (subject) with my child.

Give them about two minutes each on this exercise, then say, **"OK, I want each of you to take turns role-playing. One of you will speak and the other will actively listen. The person speaking has the option of the following subjects:**
- **What I did in the last 48 hours (as many details as possible)**
- **The funniest moment or event in my life**
- **A vacation that will always stand out"**

Explain that the "listener" cannot ask questions. All he can do is listen. When they are ready, let the first person begin. Stop him after two minutes. Then have them switch roles and continue for another two minutes. (Use the same questions as above.) When you stop them the second time, comment, **"Thanks for sharing in that exercise. Now I would like you to evaluate your own strengths and weaknesses in the role play by discussing questions 3-5 on your handout. You have only five minutes to talk about it with your partner."**

Beware of too much "dead time." Break up the discussion (even if they haven't finished) and have them turn their attention to the video.

Show the video entitled, "North." Cue it to the opening scene in which North is trying to be noticed by his parents at the dinner table. The father (Jason Alexander) and the mom (Julia Louis-Dreyfuss) ignore their son (Elijah Wood). He tries to get their attention, but they just don't listen. Finally, North fakes a heart attack. North later meets the Easter Bunny (Bruce Willis) who says, "Selfish folks. That is rough. They don't know what a good thing they got in you." North says, "Exactly." Willis comments, "Your folks are sitting on a gold mine."

After you have shown this video clip, let your participants identify some of the problems of the parents' listening skills. Then say, **"Listening needs to be active, not passive—that means putting everything aside so that we can give full eye contact and body language. We turn off our kids and can alienate them by passive listening. If you aren't sure what your kid is saying, ask, 'Could you tell me more about how you're feeling?' Listening to teens involves trying to understand what they are really saying. It means not interrupting, not giving quick advice nor changing the subject to another unresolved issue. Stick with the task at hand. Listen—not just with your head, but with your heart."**

Reveal strategy #2 on the overhead transparency—Learn to talk so your teen will listen. Ask, **"How can we talk in a way in which our teens will hear us? Let me show you a video that illustrates a negative effect on teens—a way *not* to communicate!"**

Show a clip from the video, "Dead Poets Society." Show the scene in which the father puts down the son for wanting to be in drama. The dad lectures with animosity. He delivers the ultimatum, "We are not going to let you ruin your life. Tomorrow I am withdrawing you from Weldon and enrolling you in Bradenton Military School. You are going to Harvard and you are going to be a doctor. You don't understand, Neal—you have opportunities that I've never dreamed of and I'm not going to let you waste them!" When the son tries to speak, the father gets in his face. The boy backs down and never shares his heart with him—because the father does not really care. This leads to alienation and the boy commits suicide that evening.

Comment, "**The dad had his own agenda. What are some of the issues he had?**" (Try and draw from them that the father is legalistic and rigid.) Say, "**Rules without a relationship lead to problems!**"

Continue by saying, "**Search Institute conducted a survey on whom teens wanted to hear from concerning sex. The overwhelming choice wasn't friends or even a trusted adult—it was their parents! Yet, in the survey, 13 out of 14 parents *did not* talk to their kids about sexuality. Teens *do* want us parents to talk with them. Be sensitive, honest and open. Use 'I' statements like 'I feel hurt when . . .' Don't blame or accuse. Be quick to say, 'I'm sorry.' Avoid too much lecturing, which tends to turn kids off.**

"**The verbal and nonverbal communication from a parent to a preteen or teen plays a huge role in shaping the kid's identity and how he will communicate in the future. Encourage and applaud your teens. So many of them get emotionally beaten up all day long at school. Love on them. Get them to open up by practicing reflective speaking. It makes them feel that what they have said is really important. It looks like this:**"

Teen A: "I don't know what to do about going out for cheerleading."
Parent: "You sound confused about the decision."
Teen B: "I hate school. Nothing went right today."
Parent: "What happened? Sounds like you had a rough day."

Reveal strategy # 3 on the overhead transparency—Learn to read your teen's rhythm and moods.

Say, "**Become a student of youth culture. Learn to read your teen like a book. Try and get into his world. Learn when to give space and when to express affection. Is your child an introvert needing some private time after school to unwind and disengage from people? Is your adolescent an extrovert who wants to go out with friends right after school? Read his or her rhythm and moods. Simply by being a teen, your child is learning to deal with a whole new set of emotions and chemistry going on within.**"

Refer to the different kinds of kids mentioned on the overhead. Ask parents to reflect on what kind of teens *their* children are. Then, challenge them to show their support by going to their teen's events (games, concerts, plays, etc.) Encourage them to spend time with their kids when the time is right.

♛ ♛ ♛ **CLOSING** (5 minutes)

Distribute copies of the handout on page 46 as well as writing utensils. Read together the T. A. L. K. acrostic. Then, ask participants to read the Bible verses listed from 1 John. Ask them to list one way in which they could live out each of these verses in communication with their teen(s).

Close this session by asking parents to quietly reflect on the questions listed on the handout. Challenge them to consider writing a brief sentence or two regarding how they want to improve their communication with their teen. Thank them for coming, and close in prayer. One way to do this is to ask each parent to pray for the person on his right (either aloud or silently).

Check This . . .

If you want to keep it more upbeat, show a clip from the video, "Mighty Ducks." Cue to the part in which the coach tells the boys to give up and take a "dive." Charlie refuses to cheat and says he won't play again. Coach Gordon Bombay realizes his own wrongdoing and apologizes to Charlie.

Ask, **"What were the strengths of the coach as a communicator?"** (*He apologized, he affirmed the boy and he admitted his own failure as a coach. This opened the boy up to a deeper relationship.*)

Check These Resources:

Hugging, Kevin, Parenting Adolescents, NavPress, 1990.

Habermas, Ron and Olshine, David, Tag-Team Youth Ministry, Standard Publishing, 1995.

Mueller, Walt, Understanding Today's Youth Culture, Tyndale House, 1994.

Olshine, David and Habermas, Ron. Down-But-Not-Out Parenting, Standard Publishing, 1995.

Parrott, Les, Helping the Struggling Adolescent, Zondervan, 1992.

Smith, Tim, The Relaxed Parent, Northfield Publishing, 1996.

*VIDEOS

Garrett, Dan, "Home Team" video, P. O. Box 82, West Point, GA 31833

Rice, Wayne and Davis, Ken, Youth Specialties "Understanding Your Teenager" video series, 1992. (800) 776-8008

Materials needed:
Reproducible handout on page 46 of this book; writing utensils; Bibles

When I Was a Teen
(in the Dark Ages)

1. What were your biggest complaints about your parent(s) when you were a teen? (check all that apply)

☐ out of touch   ☐ domineering
☐ uncool   ☐ they didn't trust me
☐ boring   ☐ know-it-alls
☐ legalistic   ☐ never around
☐ bad listeners   ☐ other_____

2. What subjects were you able to discuss with your parent (s) as a teen? (check all that apply)
☐ friends   ☐ sports   ☐ opposite sex   ☐ school   ☐ drugs
☐ music   ☐ very little   ☐ movies and TV   ☐ none of the above   ☐ other_____

3. When I shared something important with my parent(s), they normally . . . (check all that apply)
☐ read the newspaper   ☐ gave me full eye contact   ☐ told me not to worry about it
☐ rolled their eyes   ☐ rarely looked at me   ☐ said "huh?" after I was done
☐ gave me the "when I was your age" lecture   ☐ other_____

4. Rate your communication skills from 1-10 (when you were a teen trying to interact with your parent(s). A 1 is really bad and a 10 means super-intimate.

MY SCORE _____

Who, Me . . . Communicate?

1. I wish my teen would be able to discuss _____(subjects) with me. Explain your response.

2. I wish I could discuss _____(subjects) with my child.

3. My strengths as a communicator in this exercise were:
☐ I was honest   ☐ I had good eye contact   ☐ I was assertive   ☐ I was humorous
☐ I shared my feelings   ☐ I had good body language   ☐ other_____

4. My weakness as a listener in this exercise was:
☐ I was easily distracted   ☐ I had poor eye contact   ☐ I interrupted
☐ I wanted to talk   ☐ other_____

5. One area I'd like to improve in, especially as it relates to my kids, is . . .

Strategies for Great COMMUNICATION

1. LEARN TO LISTEN SO YOUR TEEN WILL SPEAK.

- Listening needs to be active, not passive.
- Try to understand what they are really saying.
- Don't interrupt or attempt to give quick advice.
- Don't change the subject to another unresolved issue.

2. LEARN TO TALK SO YOUR TEEN WILL LISTEN.

- Teens *do* want their parents to talk with them—but not at them.
- Be sensitive, honest and open.
- Use "I" statements like, "I feel hurt when . . ." rather than accusatory "you" statements.
- Be quick to say, "I'm sorry." Don't ignore or pounce on them verbally.
- Avoid too much lecturing. Teens turn off long lectures.
- When you give eye contact, don't stare them down or frown too much.
- Encourage and applaud them.
- Practice "reflective talking."

3. LEARN TO READ YOUR TEEN'S RHYTHM AND MOODS.

Your child has a rhythm concerning how he or she listens, talks and learns. Some kids are:
- "Analytical learners" and think deeply about most everything
- "Big picture thinkers" who see the forest but not many trees
- "Detail" people who see short-term goals but cannot see long-term
- "Visual" learners who need word pictures to bring things to life
- "Adventure" teens who love action. They discover by doing, not by listening

Adult conversation is radically different from teen talk. Adults value in-depth dialogue and want to connect. Kids don't value the kind of talk that adults do. So relax, if the conversation goes a solid ten minutes with a clear sense of continuity from the teen, a modern-day miracle has just happened! More important than anything, go to your teen's events (games, concerts, plays, etc.). Spend time with your teen when the time is right.

T. A. L. K. Is Slipping Away

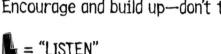

T = "TIME"
Spend quality time with your teen
—it communicates, "I love you."

A = "AFFIRM"
Encourage and build up—don't tear down.

L = "LISTEN"
Eye contact, smiles and nods let them know their ideas are valued.

K = "KNOW"
Know their world. Study them. Find ways to get inside their hearts and minds.

Look up the following verses from 1 John. List one way in which you could live out each of these verses in loving communication with your teen(s).

1 John 1:3—

1 John 3:11—

1 John 3:16–18—

1 John 5:21—

Ask yourself these questions:
1. On the average, how much time do I spend with my child each day?
2. What are some things we can do together that we will both enjoy?
3. How can I help my child express what he or she is feeling?
4. What kind of a learner is my child?
5. How can I find out more about my teen's interests?
6. What are some roadblocks that keep me from being a good listener?
7. How can I manifest love to my child that is authentic?
8. What steps do I need to take to be a better communicator?

COURSE EVALUATION

Ask your students these questions:

1. What did you like about the 1 John study?

2. What do you wish this course would have included?

3. One thing I learned from 1 John was . . .

Teacher evaluation

1. What did you find most helpful about *Actual Reality*?

2. What part of the curriculum did you find least helpful?

3. What would you like to see included in future electives?

4. Would you use curriculum like this again? Explain.

5. What were the strengths and weaknesses of the parent session?

Please return to: Dale Reeves, Acquisitions Editor of Youth Resources, Standard Publishing, 8121 Hamilton Avenue, Cincinnati, Ohio 45231